Scottish Crime

True Crime Stories

Roger Harrington

Table of Contents

Introduction

When most people around the globe think of Scotland, they think of kilts, bagpipes, and haggis — and other remnants of Scotland's infamous celtic history of being one of the toughest, and proudest, nations in the world.

More recently, Scotland has been earning a new reputation for itself on a global scale. In 2015, the United Nations conducted a survey of international crime statistics and found that Scotland currently holds the title of being the assault capital of the world, with the Edinburgh area having the highest numbers of crime, and the lowest detection statistics.

Further, the UN concluded that if you live in Scotland, you are seven times more likely to be attacked than in any other country around the world including Mexico, Colombia, and El Salvador.

While the Scottish government insists that this new title is only due to efficient reporting and detection of crimes in the country, something every country should strive for, they cannot deny that Scotland's modern history has been blood-soaked and riddled with tales of body snatching, gruesome assaults, and of course, serial murder.

Bodysnatching, Burke & Hare

The Burke and Hare murders, also known as the West Port Murders, are one of the most notorious crimes to come out of Scotland. The murderous duo William Burke and William Hare plagued Edinburgh in 1828 by taking seventeen lives all within a ten-month period. The only thing stranger than Burke and Hare committing these heinous acts in the first place was what they did with the bodies after.

In the early 19th century, Edinburgh was a leading center of anatomical study in Europe, which was largely due to the development of the University of Edinburgh. Established in 1582, the University existed across several buildings throughout Edinburgh. It wasn't until the early 19th century that the University constructed its first custom building — the Old College.

While today this building now functions as the University of Edinburgh's School of Law, its first forte was teaching medicine, and more importantly anatomy, taking over for the Edinburgh College of Surgeons and Barbers, which was granted permission for human dissections in 1506, the only College to be granted such permission in the UK for almost 40 years.

The Old College building included an anatomy theatre — a lecture hall designed especially for dissections of human cadavers. The anatomy theatre included a large tunnel that went beneath some of Edinburgh's busiest streets to a nearby house. It's soul purpose – to discreetly deliver cadavers to the theatre.

During the height of anatomical study in Edinburgh, several of the world's most famous practitioners of medicine flocked to the University to study and learn more about the human body. However, this surge of activity led to one major deficit that was hard to make up for – a lack of available human cadavers.

At the time, dissections of human cadavers were only permitted on the bodies of those who had been sentenced to death or dissection by the Scottish courts. The distinction between the two sentences was slight, but important.

The bodies of those who were sentenced to dissection automatically became the property of the surgeons who worked for the Edinburgh College for Surgeons and later for the University of Edinburgh; however, the bodies of those who had been only sentenced to death remained the property of the criminal's family.

The sentence to death did still grant surgeons permission to dissect the cadavers however, so many surgeons employed agents who would try to strike a deal with those condemned to death prior to their execution. Those who agreed to sign over rights to their bodies would receive money for debts or finer clothes for their execution. If the agent was unable to strike a bargain with the condemned, they would try again later with the family once the body had been handed over.

Only the worst of the worst received a sentence of dissection over a sentence of death. The added sentence of dissection was reserved for those who the courts deemed deserving of a fate worse than death as all dissections were performed publicly and were usually followed by public exhibition of the dissected cadaver. Originally, dissection became the Scottish court's less degrading replacement for hanging, quartering, and drawing the country's most dangerous criminals.

Later, it also replaced the punishment of hanging in chains, where a condemned murderer would be placed in a cage and left until their tarred bodies began to fall to pieces.

While many people were sentenced to death, only few were sentenced to dissection, and it was often difficult for agents to strike deals for cadavers due to what was thought to be the degrading nature of public dissection and exhibition of the corpses.

These factors led to the major deficit of cadavers in the anatomical center of Europe. This deficit led to many shady dealings between surgeons and the now-emerging underground sub-culture of body snatchers and resurrection men across Scotland and the UK.

Body snatching across Scotland and the UK rose dramatically in the 19th century to solve a major supply and demand problem that occurred with the rise of anatomical study in Edinburgh. Body snatching became an easy way to make money for those who didn't mind getting their hands, or their souls, a bit dirty.

There were two common methods of body snatching: the direct method and the tunnel method. The direct method was more common when the rise of body snatching first began. Body snatchers, or resurrection men, would dig a hole at the head of a recently dug grave until they hit the coffin.

They would then pry open the coffin and tie a rope around the corpse. When they certain the rope was secure, they would then use it to drag the corpse to the Earth's surface.

The tunnel method of body snatching was devised after the practice became more popular. It took more time, but left less tangible proof that the crime had been committed. With this method, body snatchers would dig an underground tunnel to the coffin from about four feet away.

They would pull the coffin to the tunnel's start, usually about the size of a manhole cover, and remove the body from there using a rope. Because the evidence that the grave had been dug up was so far from the grave itself, families were less likely to notice that their loved ones were missing when they visited.

Even though body snatchers took measures to conceal their actions, they had little to worry about if they were caught. Interfering with graves was only a misdemeanor crime in Scotland during the early 1800's, as long as they weren't taking any jewelry or valuables from the coffins resurrection men avoided felony charges.

Misdemeanors were punishable but only by small fines or short-term imprisonment. As a bonus, with the medical schools running a yearly deficit of approximately 450 cadavers, body snatching was often considered to be a necessary crime. It generally went unpunished by law enforcement. All the resurrection men really had to worry about was the families of those they snatched from the Earth.

Burke and Hare weren't interested in body snatching, but they were interested in making money from the surgeons who were desperate for cadavers to study. The duo found a new way to produce bodies for sale besides digging them up from their final resting places. Instead of stealing dead bodies, they would simply make new ones.

Despite being a leader in the study of medicine and anatomy, Edinburgh was a rough town in the 1820's. The city was flooded by all kinds of men, women, and children who were seeking refuge from the extreme poverty that plagued Northern

Ireland and the Scottish Highlands at the time. Edinburgh particularly had a reputation abroad for being a city of opportunity, but many migrants found quite the opposite to be true shortly after arriving. Women often turned to prostitution and men would find work doing labor of one kind or another.

In the mid-1820's, William Hare was one of these such migrants who moved to Edinburgh looking for a new start. He moved into a lodging house in the West Port area of Edinburgh where he struggled to pay his rent. While living in this house, Hare met Margaret Laird, his landlord's wife.

After only a few short months of living in the Laird's lodging house, Hare was evicted after getting into an altercation with Margaret's husband. Strangely, about a month later Laird's husband was found dead. Hare immediately married Margaret and began running the lodging house as his own.

Hare's new lodging house held both visitors to the area and long-term residents. Like Hare himself when he was living there as a mere tenant, they were the poorest of the poor. Many were away from their families, scoping out Edinburgh for work or other opportunities before moving the rest of their families in, and many more were prostitutes and laborers who would spend their day struggling to make even the cheapest rent.

Hare met William Burke only a year or two after he assumed ownership of the lodging house. Burke moved into the house with his wife, Helen McDougal. The pair got along famously and would often spend their evenings discussing current events and other news in the house's parlor or one of their private rooms.

Soon, Burke became an influential figure in Hare's life. Although he never formally owned any portion of Hare's house, Burke began helping with the day-to-day business of the house. They made decisions about the business together, consulting with each other on all personal and professional manners. When it was later discovered that Burke and Hare had been committing murders, there was little surprise that they had been acting as a team, not individually.

Despite his business running well, Hare was not a wealthy man. He relied heavily on his tenants and guests paying on time and in full. Any late payments meant that Hare would also be paying his rent late that month. This put Hare in a particularly difficult spot in 1827 when an elderly man by the name of Old Donald died in his room in Hare's lodging while still owing Hare over four dollars in rent.

When Old Donald's body was discovered by Hare he instantly began plotting a way to ensure he would be paid the rent he was still owed, and with Burke's help, the pair pulled off the plot with extreme ease.

Burke and Hare decided the best way for Hare to receive the money he was still owed by Old Donald was to sell his corpse for dissection. It was an obvious choice, and one that was morally justifiable. As his unpaid landlord, Hare was due a portion of Old Donald's estate. It just so happened that Old Donald's entire estate was himself.

The pair weighed down Old Donald's coffin with stones before it was delivered for his burial and they brought the corpse itself right to the University where they were commended for the freshness of the body. The surgeons paid almost twice the amount that Hare was owed. It was the fastest cash either of them had ever made.

About a month after they had sold their first corpse to the surgeons, Burke and Hare spotted another opportunity to repeat their seemingly flawless plot. This time, in the form of a tenant of Hare's coming down with an extreme illness. The pair decided they would again wait for this tenant to die, weigh down his coffin, and sell his corpse for dissection.

However, this time their plan hit a snag. Although the tenant was incredibly ill, he was taking a long time to die. The pair worried that he would start to recover, or his family would come to take care of him, before they had the chance to cash in on his death. They needed to act fast to secure what they saw as their investment — they would screw fate and kill the man themselves.

Working as a team, Burke and Hare sedated the ill tenant with whiskey so the man would be less likely to cause a struggle or make a scene. They then suffocated him by covering his nose and mouth while physically restraining him. In order to fully suffocate the man, they would have had to have held this position for around five minutes.

Although to most people, this would be a very traumatic five minutes, Burke and Hare found a passion in killing by suffocation. It became their preferred method of killing. Suffocation did not leave and physical signs of murder to be discovered by the anatomists who would soon be dissecting the body. As long as they weren't caught in the act, their murders would remain undetectable. This method of murder is still known today in Scotland as Burking.

Altogether, Burke and Hare killed seventeen men and women in this fashion — the majority of which were completely healthy at the time. One of their most notorious victims was Mary, a beautiful young woman who had caught the eye of Burke one morning.

After chatting for a while, Mary agreed to have morning drinks with Burke — a mistake she would spend the short remainder of her life regretting. After getting the woman fairly drunk, Burke brought her to his room at his lodging house. He waited until she passed out and then took the opportunity to suffocate her.

Because Mary was highly inebriated, Burke was able to commit the murder alone. Hare was not needed to physically restrain the victim to prevent struggling like he did in their other murders. Burke only called for Hare to assist him after she was dead. They needed to undress and clean the body to prepare it for sale.

Mary's body was not immediately dissected by the surgeons who had purchased her for a whopping ten pounds — the most money Burke and Hare received from the sale of any of their victims. She was instead preserved in whiskey for several months and then carefully dissected.

The reason for this was after being preserved in whiskey; a dissected body could be examined by students for several months afterwards instead of simply used as a one-time demonstration. It is believed that Mary's body was chosen for preservation because the surgeon who bought her corpse was quite taken with her beauty.

The surgeon, Dr Knox, had also had several sketches of Mary's body made in a variety of poses before her body was placed in the preservative. Two of these sketches remain in the property of the University of Edinburgh today.

At the height of their murder spree, Burke and Hare was murdering and selling a body every two weeks. They took care to pray on the loneliest lodgers or strangers on the street that they could find. They were the easiest targets as if the victim had no family around, Burke and Hare would have less people to fool, and no one to compete with for the body. They preyed on prostitutes, drifters, and the old and lonely.

They had been completely blinded by money. At the rate they were killing, the pair began to each make a year's wages in a month. They had also managed to evade any sense of detection by law enforcement, they were seemingly invincible.

Because the surgeons who bought Burke and Hare's bodies were so desperate for cadavers, they never asked where they came from, and never reported the men when the bodies seemed a bit too fresh — something surgeons at the time were morally, but not legally, obliged to do at the time. The Police didn't know a crime was being committed, let alone that Burke and Hare were behind it.

The confidence Burke and Hare gained from their seemingly undetectable crimes began a violent crash however when Burke met their final victim, an old woman by the name of Mrs. Campbell or Docherty, in a grog shop. After gaining her trust, Burke took her to his home, gave her more drinks, and along with Hare killed her.

At this time, Burke had made enough money from his business of selling corpses that he no longer needed to live in Hare's lodging house. He had moved into his own home down the road with his wife. Burke had become so comfortable killing that he forgot that two of his wife's relatives were staying in Burke's home the day he brought home and murdered Mrs. Campbell or Docherty. This mistake was ultimately the pair's undoing.

The morning after Mrs. Docherty was murdered; Burke's relatives had the misfortune of discovering her body under a bed in one of Burke's spare rooms. Shocked by this gruesome find, they immediately went to the Police. By the time the police arrived, however, the body was gone.

It didn't take long for the Police to suspect that the body may have been sold for dissection, and they quickly located the body in the office of Dr. Knox, a favorite surgeon of Burke and Hare who was known to pay best for the freshest cadavers. The body was identified by Burke's relatives and Burke was quickly taken into custody. By November 2, 1828, Burke, Hare, and their wives were all four in police custody.

But the path to justice was to take a strange turn when a month later Hare agreed to testify against court in exchange for immunity for himself and his wife, who no doubt had been involved in the scheme along with Burke's wife as well. For the Scottish Police, this was a deal they couldn't turn down.

With little to go on besides the fact that Mrs. Docherty's body had first been discovered in Burke's house, the Scottish Police were going to have a tough time proving that Burke and

Hare had committed wrongdoing, let alone that they had killed seventeen people. They agreed to grant Hare and his wife immunity in exchange for his testimony. At the time, having one killer die for their crimes was better than none.

The story of Burke and Hare's murders and subsequent arrests spread like the plague across Scotland and the UK. Burke's trial was to be the trial of the decade, and all of Scotland's best lawyers took part. Although Mrs. Docherty's murder was the subject of the trial, Hare publicly confessed that he and Burke had murdered sixteen others together.

The police were able to confirm most of Hare's claims before the trial by recovering several personal objects of his victims from the office of Dr. Knox and several other surgeons around Edinburgh. To most people attending the trial, Hare's details were a complete shock. It was the first trial of a serial killer the country has ever witnessed, and it clearly left a mark.

Burke was unsurprisingly found to be guilty of murdering Mrs. Docherty and was given the same, albeit ironic, sentence given to all murders at the time — he was sentenced to dissection. Burke's wife, who had also been charged with murder, was found to be not proven — a sentence popular in Scotland even today which neither proclaims innocence nor denies guilt.

When the day of Burke's execution arrived, he was publicly hanged in one of the most attended executions in Scotland's history and his body was delivered to the University of Edinburgh where it was publicly dissected. As of 2016, Burke's skeleton still hangs in the Anatomical Museum of Edinburgh Medical School.

While Burke's life ended in 1827, their story and influence stood for several generations. If you ever visit Edinburgh, you will encounter many Burke and Hare themed tours and souvenirs. The killing duo is Edinburgh's Jack the Ripper. Their story resonates throughout the city now almost as strong as it did in the 1820's — and it did resonate back then. Burke and Hare's story was one of the most influential justifications for the 1832 Anatomy Act.

Through its gruesome details, Burke and Hare's murders brought awareness to the public surrounding the great need and importance of bodies being used for medical research. The Anatomy Act of 1832 made it possible for people to legally donate their bodies to science in the hopes of closing the obscene cadaver deficit growing medical schools across the UK were facing, something that made it possible for a black market for corpses to not only become possible, but to also thrive.

While Burke and Hare are one of Scotland's most notorious killing duos, Robert Black, from Grangemouth, Scotland has built his reputation for bringing death to wherever he visited all on his own.

Robert Black
Grangemouth

Robert Black was a Scottish paedophile and serial killer who was convicted of the kidnap, sexual assault, rape, and murder of four girls all aged between five and eleven in the 1980's. He was also convicted of sexually assaulting several other young women throughout his lifetime.

Nicknamed Smelly Bobby due to his poor hygiene habits, Black worked alone as a van driver, which allowed him to spread his terror all across the UK; however, his crimes began during his bizarre childhood in Grangemouth, Scotland.

Robert Black was born in April of 1947 to a young, unwed Mother who could only stand to raise the child for six months before placing him into foster care. Although his new parents, the Tulips, loved him very much, Black was continually haunted by the abandonment he felt from never knowing his true parents.

Growing up in the Scottish Highlands, Black soon became an aggressive child — he was anti-social, prone to tantrums and a target for his school bullies. He loved his foster mother deeply and adopted her last name as his own. Although troubled, his younger years would be some of the most peaceful of his life. When Black was eleven, his foster mother died, leaving Black to feel more isolated and alone than ever before.

Not only was young Robert Black dealing with intense feelings of isolation, he was also dealing with bizarre sexual fantasies that had already began to plague his mind. After comparing genitals with a female peer at the age of five, Black decided he had been born incorrectly; he should have been born a girl. He began fixating on the idea of female genitalia and would frequently dress up in female clothing.

After the death of his foster mother, Black was sent away again, and again. His aggressive nature and developing psychological issues that were already presenting themselves meant that no foster family was able to keep the young boy in their care for long. After one foster parent reported catching Black sexually fondling a

young girl in a public restroom, Black was
sent to a children's home.

Here, Black's troubles continued. He started
regularly flashing his female peers and
committed several other offences. During
one incident, Black was caught forcibly
removing a young girl's underwear. After it
was clear Black would be unable to
assimilate with his peers in a mixed-gender
environment, he was sent to a strict, all-male
boarding house just six miles East of
Edinburgh. Here, in the Red House Care
Home, staff was sure they would be able to
subdue Black's behavior and break the
troubling behavioral pattern he had begun to
develop.

While Black lived in the Red House Care Home in the Scottish Highlands, he committed very few offences. He had limited contact with young females, as it was an all-male institution, so the only way he was able to fulfill his fantasies was in his mind. Many horrors were still committed behind closed doors in the home, though. They just weren't at the hands of Black himself — they at the hands of the staff.

Black was continuously sexually abused during his stay in the Red House Care Home. He was forced to fondle and perform fellatio on members of the home's all-male staff. While he was now being placed in the shoes of his own victims, he was still unable to feel sympathy for them, even though he was outraged at what was happening to him — a clear sign of psychopathy.

Black became a part of the sexual abuse ring in the Red House Care Home through a very troubling recommendation system — something that was later found to be a common trend in sexual abuse rings in care homes for children. When a child who was being sexually abused left the home, they were forced to recommend another child to take their place when they were gone.

This left them feeling guilty enough to keep their abuse a secret. If the young child felt like they had committed a wrong, they wouldn't want to implicate themselves, and would keep quiet. Black tried to reach out to his social workers and have himself reassigned to a new care home, but his social workers decided to keep him there.

Likely, they believed he wanted to be reassigned to another mixed-gender home where he could have contact with young girls again. Based on his background, and his new reduced sexually deviancy, they decided to keep with what seemed to be working.

Black's sexual abuse continued for three years, during which time Black continually appealed to his social workers to have him moved. Black's sexual abuse finally came to an end when the abusive staff member died of natural causes. Black still felt uncomfortable staying in the setting of the worst years of his life. Every corner of the house brought back painful memories that only added to the already troubling relationship Black had with his sexual identity and fantasies.

Black was eventually reassigned to another all-male care home in Greenock, Scotland. Here, Black was allowed more freedom. He hadn't been able to commit an offence in some time, so it looked like he was finally on the straight and narrow.

Black was permitted to find work outside of the home as he was no longer in school. He quickly found work in the local town as a butcher's delivery boy, a job he quite liked as it gave him access to the general public and required him to visit people in their homes.

It didn't take long for Black to get back up to his old tricks—he later admitted to police that if he discovered a young girl at home alone, he would sexually fondle her before leaving. When police asked him how many girls he was able to fondle through this motive of opportunity, Black estimated between 30-40. This was thought to be a rather conservative estimate. Black was sixteen at the time.

The same summer Black moved out of the Red House Care Home, he received his first criminal conviction for a stunningly horrific stunt. Black was walking through a children's park one night when he noticed a seven-year-old girl alone on the swings. Black approached the girl and told her he had found a litter of kittens in a nearby abandoned air-raid shelter. When the young girl followed him into the isolated space Black grabbed her by the throat and choked her until she lost consciousness. He then masturbated over her body.

The young girl was found hours later crying hysterically next to the shelter by her parents who were worried when she hadn't returned home when the street lights came on. Thanks to the girl's statements, and several witness statements, it took police only a day to find and arrest Black for the crime. Because of Black's history in the foster care system, it was decided that he should undergo a psychiatric exam prior to appearing in court.

During this exam, Black was able to convince the psychiatrist that this had been an isolated offence and he was not likely to reoffend. Black was still only sixteen at the time and appeared to be nothing but a troubled youth. Not wanting to stunt his potential further, it was decided that Black would be pardoned for the offence and no other actions or treatment would be required.

While he was not charged for kidnapping and sexually abusing the young girl, he was removed from his new care home and dropped by his social workers. He was now all on his own. Black decided to move back to Grangemouth, the city of his birth, where he rented a room from an elderly couple and found work with a construction supply company.

Conveniently, his new landlords had a nine-year-old granddaughter who visited the home frequently. Black found several opportunities to be left alone with the child as the elderly couple were all too trusting of the young man. Black used these opportunities to molest the girl, and when his landlords finally became aware, they were worried about causing their granddaughter more trauma and chose not to report Black. They settled with evicting the heinous Black.

When Black began looking for new accommodations, he specifically sought a landlord with young children. He found a room for rent in a nearby town in the home of a married couple who had a seven-year-old daughter. Although the room was shabby, Black was pleased with his new landlords who asked him if he liked babysitting when interviewing him for the room. His answer was of course yes.

Black stayed in this house for nearly a year. When his landlords eventually realized that he had been molesting their daughter while watching her, they reported him to police. Black was subsequently charged with three counts of indecent assault against a child. Black, still a minor at the time, pleaded guilty to all charges and was sent to a borstal—a juvenile detention system that was popular for offenders under 21 in the UK.

Borstals were used in the UK to separate youths from the older convicts they would encounter in adult prisons. The theory behind borstals was to protect youths from falling victim to brutal beatings and sexual assault in prison as their young age made them easy targets, and to help rehabilitate young offenders who were seen as still having time to correct their ways before committing to a life of crime.

Borstals attempted to rehabilitate young offenders by introducing them to a life of routine, discipline, and authority — something many young offenders such as Black had never really experienced before. Borstals were thought to be more educational than punitive, and their inmates were assigned a schedule that included regular work periods and blocks of time set out for education.

In theory, borstals were a place for misguided youth to see the error in their ways and learn to correct them before it was too late — in practice, they were anything but. Overwhelming statements from inmates subjected to borstals reveal that physical abuse was rampant among officers, despite corporal punishment allowing being allowed under extreme circumstances, and even then required an official magistrate to oversee the procedure. Abuse between inmates, both physical and sexual, was also reportedly rampant in borstals.

The borstal system was officially abolished in 1982, nearly a hundred years since its inception. It was becoming clear to everyone that borstals were too under regulated, and were no longer a humane place to send young offenders. In his essay The A-Z of Law and Disorder, celebrated crime author Bernard O'Mahoney quoted one investigation that described borstals as being not much more than breeding grounds for bullies and psychopaths.

The system was replaced by well-regulated youth detention centers, which were reserved for the worst of the worst youths. Most crimes that would normally have resulted in sentencing to a borstal were instead sentenced to community service or correctional therapy programs.

Black spent a year in the Polmont Borstal in Brightons, a Scottish town just outside of Falkirk. The Polmont Borstal specialized in rehabilitating and educating what was seen as the most dangerous youth offenders in Scotland at the time. Not much is known about Black's time in Polmont.

Despite openly discussing intimate details about his adolescent years to criminologists while serving life in prison later in his life, including details about his sexual abuse at the Red House Care Home, Black refused to discuss his experiences at the Polmont Borstal, leaving criminologists to speculate on the horrors and brutalities he must have suffered over the course of that year.

Shortly after his release from the borstal, Black decided to leave Scotland, the country that had imprisoned him in his darkest hell. He relocated to London, where he found work that would soon bring him back to his country of birth, and across the rest of the UK.

Black moved into the attic of Edward and Kathy Rayson, a Scottish couple he had met while playing darts at a local pub. The Rayson's enjoyed having Black as a tenant; they had little to complain about besides his poor hygiene, which wasn't much of a problem as Black was very reclusive and seldom seen by the couple. Black had also begun working as a delivery driver for a poster company, so he would spend large periods of time making deliveries across the UK. Black lived with the Rayson's until his final arrest in 1990 - an eighteen year stay.

Black began to thrive in London; he had found his place in the world. Working as a delivery driver allowed him to feel unrestricted for the first time in years. The frequent travel gave him a sense of freedom and distracted him from his lack of family or close friends. He also made several connections in London including a bookshop owner who supplied him child pornography.

When Black first began to collect this material, he stuck to magazines and photographs which he kept amongst the uncountable number of photos he took himself of children playing in parks or swimming in pools. When photographs no longer were able to satisfy his needs, he began to purchase videos depicting the graphic sexual assault of children. His landlords, the Rayson's, had no idea what was going on above their heads each night.

In the catalogue of crime, there is no more abhorrent in the eyes of the law or the public than the murder of a child. When you add a sexual motive, police will leave no stone unturned in the search for the killer. So when nine-year-old Jennifer Cardy was reported missing on August 12, 1981, police sprang into action, launching a county-wide search for the girl.

Jennifer Cardy lived in Ballinderry, in Northern Ireland, with her family. She had celebrated her ninth birthday just two weeks before her disappearance. On her last day alive, an idyllic sunny summer's day, Cardy had left her home around 1:30pm to ride her bike a few blocks over to a friend's house. When she did not return home several hours later, Cardy's parent's phoned her friend's house only to learn she had never arrived.

The police were unsuccessful in finding Cardy's body or any witnesses that could recall seeing the girl that day. They did however find her bike less than a mile from the Cardy's home with its kickstand down. This suggested to police and Cardy's parents that shortly into her ride, she was stopped and lured away from her bike. It suggested a kidnapping. Six days after they reported her missing, Cardy's parents had their worst fears confirmed when two duck hunters discovered Jennifer Cardy's body in a reservoir a few county's over.

Cardy's body told a story to police — she had been strangled with a ligature sexually abused, and thrown into the water while still breathing. Her official cause of death was drowning. Cardy had been wearing a watch the day she disappeared that had been stopped at 5:40pm suggesting she had been thrown into the reservoir around four hours after she left home. Four grueling hours of being constrained in Black's van while he drove away from the scene until he eventually stopped to strangle and abuse the young girl, finishing only disposing her body.

The location of Cardy's body also helped police begin to identify the man they were now eagerly searching for. The abduction site and murder site had been miles apart, but the abduction and murder had occurred only hours apart. He had to have a way to conceal the young girl in an unrecognizable vehicle.

As well, the reservoir was located beside a highway that was frequented by long-distance delivery drivers, not local traffic as it connected major cities but did not cross through them. All these details led investigators believe there was a good chance Cardy's killer frequently travelled long distances by van or truck for work, although they did not focus solely on this idea at the time.

It would be almost 30 years until Black was found guilty for the murder of Jennifer Cardy. While she was his first murder victim, she was the last he was convicted for.

A year after he murdered nine-year-old Jennifer Cardy, Robert Black, now 35, found himself driving along the Anglo-Scottish border with eleven-year-old Susan Maxwell tied up and shoved in a sleeping bag in the back of his van.

Susan Maxwell had been walking home from playing tennis in the nearby courts across the border in Coldstream. She had last been spotted crossing the River Tweed at 4:30pm. She was thought to have been kidnapped shortly after she traversed the river's bridge.

The day after Maxwell was reported missing by her mother; police launched a full-scale search on both sides of the border. At the height of this search, over 300 officers had dedicated themselves, alongside cadaver dogs, to finding the eleven-year-old girl. The search turned up nothing. Two days after he had kidnapped Maxwell, Black had disposed of her body in a heavily-forested area on the side of a highway in Staffordshire, England — 264 miles from where he abducted her.

Maxwell had spent over 24-hours in Black's van. He kept her while he completed deliveries in Edinburgh, Dundee, and Glasgow. He was on his way back to his home in London when he finally made the time to abuse and murders the young girl. Her kidnapping had likely been a crime of opportunity; it was a chance Black couldn't pass up despite being in the middle of work at the time.

Maxwell's body was eventually found a month after she went missing by a driver of an 18-wheeler who had stopped on the side of the road to urinate in the forested area. Her body had been in an advanced state of decomposition, making it difficult for investigators to determine the exact cause, time, or date of her death. What was evident was that she had been bound, gagged, and assaulted by her kidnapper. She was fully clothed minus her underwear, which had been neatly folded and placed underneath her body.

Susan Maxwell and Jennifer Cardy had been abducted, sexually assaulted, and murdered by the same man, but investigators working on either case had yet to discover this fact. Although it was clear in both cases that the abductor had been able to transport his victims long distances, circumstances still made it difficult for the cases to be connected. Robert Black would take one more victim before investigators began to realize they had a serial killer on their hands.

Caroline Hogg was Black's third, and youngest, victim. The five-year-old was playing outside her home in an Edinburgh suburb on July 8, 1983 when Black approached the girl and offered to bring her to a nearby playground and Fun City, a nearby amusement park. Black spent an inordinate amount of time with Hogg before entrapping the girl is his van and driving away.

He was spotted by several eyewitnesses, many of whom were children themselves, sitting with Hogg on park benches and paying for her to go on rides at Fun City. When witnesses saw Hogg leaving Fun City with the man they presumed was her father, they said the young girl looked scared.

Hogg's body was found discarded in a ditch ten days after she disappeared, 310 miles away from her home. Like in Susan Maxwell's case, investigators had a tough time determining the exact cause and time of Hogg's death due to the advanced state of composition of her body.

Because of the distance between where she lived and where her body was found, they knew that she had had to have been in the possession of her abductor for more than 24-hours. On top of that, an entomologist that had been called in to assist with the case determined that Hogg's body could not have been placed where it had been found before July 12, four days after she went missing and four days before she was found. Although it was unclear what she had had to endure during that time, sexual abuse at the minimum was a given as she was found completely naked.

Susan Maxwell and Caroline Hogg's cases were both highly publicized, putting pressure on UK investigators. Investigator's failed to connect Maxwell's murder with Jennifer Cardy's until 2009, but after Hogg's body was discovered just 24 miles away from where Maxwell's was, they instantly began to investigate her murder as part of a series.

One the main factors that led to the connection between the two cases was the fact that distance had played a large part in both murders. Police were convinced that the man who murdered both children drove a delivery van or lorry for work across the UK.

In an effort to focus on capturing the paedophillic serial killer UK investigators now believed was plaguing their country, a coordinated task force was assembled. At the time, the information from both murders had been stored and organized using an index card system, however, with over half a million index cards being used for the

Maxwell murder itself, investigators soon became overwhelmed.

Cross-checking simple information became an incredibly difficult task which caused major delays in the case. It was soon decided that the investigation needed to bring in new technology if they were ever going to find their man, so they entered all the information pertaining to both Maxwell and Hogg's cases into the HOLMES 2 database, a system that had been invented to aid British police in capturing the infamous Yorkshire Ripper. Ironically, it would be in Yorkshire that Black would strike next.

Late March of 1968, Black kidnapped ten-year-old Sarah Harper from Morely, a suburb in Leeds, as she walked home from buying a loaf of bread at a local corner store. She had been gone for less than an hour before her mother reported her missing to the West Yorkshire Police who immediately went to work searching nearby areas and going door-to-door to look for the girl. Despite their immediate efforts, they were unable to find a single trace of Harper, who was riding in the back of Black's van concealed in a sleeping bag by then.

Black kept Harper alive for only eight hours, but during this time he sexually assaulted the young girl so severely that the pathologist who performed her autopsy described the internal damage as being "simply terrible." After he had finished raping the girl, he brutally beat her around her head and face, rendering her unconscious. He then threw her body into the River Trent, where her partially-dressed, bound and gagged body was discovered sixteen days later.

Sarah Harper's murder was connected to Maxwell and Hogg's after police received matching descriptions of a man driving a white van near both the abduction and disposal sites around the times that matched the evidential times. As well, a pattern had begun to develop between all three victims.

They had all been pre-pubescent, white females who had been abducted from the area surrounding the border between Northern England and Scotland, who had also all been found dead somewhere along the route back to London. As well, little effort had been taken to conceal either bodies. The details surrounding Harper's murder was added to the task force's database.

After murdering Sarah Harper, Robert Black fell into a bit of a slump. He attempted to abduct 15-year-old Theresa Thornhill in Radford, but was foiled when the girl fought back and managed to get the attention of her boyfriend who was nearby. Thornhill was under five feet tall, making her appear younger than fifteen.

Black likely thought she was closer in age to his previous victims and had underestimated her ability to fight back. Both Thornhill and her boyfriend were able to describe her abductor in a way that matched previous eye witness statements in earlier cases. This led to the attempted abduction being linked back to Black after his capture.

Black was shaken up by his failed abduction of Theresa Thornhill. He waited almost two years before trying again. This time, he attempted to abduct a six-year-old girl in broad daylight from her yard in a friendly looking neighborhood in Stow. This attempted abduction would be the end of Black's crime spree.

By chance, a neighbor of the young girl, 53-year-old David Herkes, was outside mowing his lawn when he noticed a van pull up to his neighbor's yard. The driver got out and began to clean his windshield so Herkes thought nothing of it. As he went back to his lawn, he happened to notice the young girl's feet rise off the sidewalk out of the corner of his eye and a chill ran through his body. He immediately realized that he was witnessing child abduction so he noted the van's license plate number and ran inside to call the police as the van sped away.

Although it took less than six minutes for police to arrive on the scene, the van was nowhere to be seen so police began their usual routine of knocking on doors and collecting potential witness statements. They went up to Herkes' house and began asking him to describe the vehicle when, in a navigational error made by Black, the van drove by behind the police.

When Herkes identified the van, an officer jumped in front of the moving vehicle, causing Black to swerve and crash. They immediately opened the back doors of the van and found the six-year-old bound, gagged, and concealed inside a sleeping bag. Black was immediately arrested and charged with the attempted kidnapping.

When the information regarding this attempted abduction was entered into the task force's database, like all child-related crimes were at the time, it didn't take long before investigators realized Black was the man they had been looking for. Black was transferred to an Edinburgh prison where he stood trial for the attempted abduction.

He was found guilty and given a life sentence. This gave investigator's all the time they needed to continue to try and convict Black of his crimes all across the UK, all of which he was found guilty for. The last trail pertaining to his crimes was for the murder of Jennifer Cardy in 2009.

While incarcerated, Black was visited by several criminologists who were working to understand the minds of serial killers to gain a better insight into psychopathy and what leads these people to kill. During these interviews, Black was surprisingly candid, divulging details about his fantasies and crimes as well as events in his past that he believes led to him becoming a paedophile.

He also admitted to keeping trophies from his murders, clothing from his victims, which he would rub on his body and masturbate with in an attempt to feel closer to those that he, spent what he called his tender moments with. Black did not express any regret or sadness for his crimes at any point.

Robert Black's crimes were made all the more horrifying due to the young age of his victims. Black, however, isn't the only one who has targeted Scotland's most vulnerable population. In 2014, Rachel and Nyomi Fee were charged with neglecting, abusing, and murdering their son Liam Fee, who was only two years old when he died, in a case that shook the country by its callousness and barbarity.

The Liam Fee Case

Liam Fee was born in 2012 in Fife, Scotland where he spent his whole life. He was the youngest of three boys, all of whom lived with their mother, Rachel Fee, and her civil partner Nyomi. Liam's life was short, but filled with tragedy. His mother and her partner constantly abused the boy and his two brothers — even outsiders of the family could tell something was wrong. When Liam was brought to daycare, the workers would often notice strange bruises and scratches all over Liam's body.

When asked about these injuries, Rachel would blame her other sons or say they were merely the superficial evidence of an active childhood. Another startling fact to daycare workers were that Liam would burst into tears the second either Rachel or Nyomi entered the room to bring him home at the end of the day. He never cried when they dropped him off.

While many who came into contact with Liam knew something not quite right was going on at home, no one could have predicted the reality of the situation.

Liam Fee died of a ruptured heart due to blunt force trauma to his chest and abdomen when he was two years old. Beyond his internal injuries, the coroner of the case was startled to discover over thirty external injuries including a broken thigh and arm; both unreported and untreated despite being several days old.

In court, the coroner described Liam's injuries as being similar to those of someone who had been in a severe car crash. When Rachel and Nyomi were asked by police how Liam died, they provided a startling answer — one of their other sons had suffocated his brother.

The allegations that one of Rachel and Nyomi's sons had killed his own brother was immediately suspicious to police. When investigators tried to talk to the young boy, he was wary and withdrawn — he acted more like a victim himself than an overly aggressive brother who had just killed someone else in his family. Further, the boy, like Liam, was also covered in unexplainable bruises and scratches.

Police quickly decided that there was much more to this story then they were being told so they launched a full investigation into how Liam Fee died. This led them into the Fee household where they made a startling discovery that instantly led to the arrest of both Rachel and Nyomi.

To investigators, the Fee household resembled a torture chamber more than a loving, caring household. They found several cage-like structures in the house, one under a mattress on a bed frame, and locks on the fridge. Immediately, they began to fear the worse—Liam died at the hands of his abusive parents, and he wasn't the only victim in the house.

Following the search of the Fee household, Liam's two brothers were separated and put into protective custody. Investigators needed to know the extent of abuse that was happening in the house, and they needed it to be unquestionable. The best way to do this was by interviewing both boys separately and finding the common denominations in their stories.

The interviews conducted with Liam's siblings showed a horrifying life, and gave deep insight into how Liam spent his last few days alive: alone and in pain. Tapings of each boy's interviews were shown to the court during Liam's murder trial, and was thought to be the most damning evidence presented against the two women, although investigators had easily discovered plenty of damning circumstantial evidence.

Liam Fee's brothers were interviewed by a public protection officer, who specialized in interviewing children, alongside a social worker who had slowly won the trust of the boys. She empathized with their situation and was kind to them, something the boys hadn't experience much of before. Separately, both boys told the social worker and protection officer the extent of Rachel and Nyomi's abuse.

All three boys were regularly denied access to their basic needs such as food, water, and a bathroom. If the boys had an accident, they were forced to take cold showers or would be beaten as a punishment. The fridge was kept locked at night so the boys couldn't sneak a snack when they were starving.

If they boys begged for food, they would be forced to eat dog excrement, and when they vomited they had to eat that as well. Liam would often be chained to the ground to limit his ability to roam the house alone. Investigators found chains secured to the floor in several rooms of the Fee's house.

One of the boys admitted he had to sleep inside the makeshift cages at night. His mother would tie him to the cage and he would spend the entire night trying not to wet himself. He recalled one night in particular where he was put in the cage while his mother watched TV.

He remembered dreaming up an escape plot where he used the bandages on his injured foot like rope to rappel out of the house's window. The other boy spoke of a time he was chained to a chair in a dark room where his mom kept pet snakes and their food — boxes of rats. He was told that the animals were trained to eat naughty boys.

He spent the night trying not to cry too loud so that the snakes wouldn't hear and come get him.

Both stories were corroborated without prompting by the other brother. In court, the interviews could not be played for more than five or six minutes at a time. Eventually, one of the jurors would ask for a break in order to compose themselves. Rachel and Nyomi never shed a tear.

Alongside the two boy's statements, Rachel and Nyomi's google searches from their phones the days before Liam died were presented. Both women had googled damning questions such as "how do you treat a broken leg," "possible injuries if you can't put pressure on a leg," "can you die from a broken bone," and, most damningly, "can wives be in prison together."

At the end of the seven week trial, both Rachel and Nyomi Fee were found guilty of the abuse and murder of Rachel's son Liam Fee. They were also found guilty of neglecting and abusing the two other boys in their care.

Both women were sentenced to life in prison, and the pair was sent to separate institutions. While they both continued to deny they had killed Liam, they did admit some guilt throughout the trial. Nyomi admitted to not seeking medical attention when she suspected that Liam had a broken leg, despite the fact that she feared he could die from the injury. Her reasoning? She didn't want Rachel to get mad and leave her. Both women maintain that one of their other boys was the one to stop Liam's heart.

Since being charged with the abuse and murder of their children in 2014, Rachel and Nyomi Fee are often thought to be the most hated parents in all of Scotland. However, the couple are receiving support from a surprising source — Liam Fee's own grandmother.

Janice Fee, Rachel's mother, has insisted to the Scottish media several times that she knows exactly what happened to Liam the night he died, and it was not Rachel's fault. Janice has spoken against the media for painting her daughter as a cruel, heartless mother, ignoring many pieces of evidence that shows how much Rachel cared for the boy.

Further, Janice argues that if Liam's abuse was as bad as his brothers and police would have the public believed, surely someone would report them before Liam died.

In reality, Liam's abuse was reported several times, but the government missed several opportunities to protect the young child. Heather Farmer, Liam's first ever babysitter, called the Scottish Childminding Association and Care Inspectorate in 2013 to report that she had witnessed bruising on several parts of Liam's body across the month that she had known him.

When a social worker visited the home, they were told that the toddler had simply bumped his head. Satisfied with this explanation, the social workers left and did not continue to investigate the household. After the investigation was closed, Farmer could no longer bear to see the young blonde-haired blue-eyed boy continue to endure physical so she told Rachel and

Nyomi she could no longer take care of the boy. She also stated that she felt like re-reporting was useless as the first social workers dismissed the abuse so easily.

Three months after Farmer had reported Liam Fee's family, Liam began attending nursery school. Just a few weeks into starting at the nursery school, the staff became concerned and again reported the Fee's for suspicion of child abuse. This time, however, they contacted social services. The social worker who was assigned to check up on the toddler was not aware that a previous report had been made due to a lack of communication in the Scottish government agencies that deal with child abuse.

Again, social workers left convinced that the marks on the child were simply due to the natural causes of childhood. A third report to social workers was made by a neighbor of the Fees who reported seeing Liam in a baby carriage looking "deathly," like he may have been drugged. This final report was made only four months before Liam was found dead and severely underweight.

In all three cases, the social workers assigned to follow up with the reports being made against the Fees were unaware of any previous reports. The Scottish government has since put in place the named person's bill, which allows government agencies dealing with children more rights to communicate with each other in hopes of preventing another heartbreaking case like Liam Fee's.

Case's like Liam Fees are beyond a doubt terrible for all involved but closure can be found when those who are responsible are punished. In Glasgow, a series of killings that happened between 1968 and 1969 remain unsolved, leaving a ghost to haunt the streets and minds of women throughout the city.

Bible John

The Bible John murders are an unsolved series of killings in Glasgow that occurred between 1968 and 1969. The name Bible John was given to the unknown killer after a witness statement claimed the man police believed to be their killer was named John and quoted the Bible frequently in conversation. The original investigation relied heavily on the same witness's statement, but as the case slowly began to crawl to a cold stop, many have wondered if the witness was as credible as she originally seemed.

In the 1960's Glasgow was a city filled street by street with exciting nightlife. Dancing was a major pastime in the city, with dance halls on every major street. But for one young woman, a taxi ride home from one of these ballrooms in October 1969 with a man she just met was destined to end in tragedy. As the cab made its way through the streets it was clear that his fate was already sealed. It seemed she'd been dancing with a killer.

Helen Puttock's body was found in the backcourt of her apartment building on October 31, 1969. She'd been out dancing with her sister Jean at the Barrowland ballroom the night before but had never quite made it to her front door although her cab had dropped her off just yards away. She'd been strangled.

Helen Puttock was a vivacious 29-year-old woman. She had two little boys and was married to George Puttock, who was in the army. The couple had just returned from a posting in Germany. Helen was an absolute bubbly character, full of life. She loved music and dancing and most of all her two young sons. The young couple was living with Helen's mother on Earl Street in Glasgow.

On the night she was murdered, Puttock was out on the town with her sister Jean. They went into Schiller's Tavern and had a few drinks before heading to the now infamous Barrowland ballroom. During the course of the evening, Helen and her sister Jean had met two men who became their companions for the night. At the end of the evening, the man interested in Jean made his way home while the other shared a taxi with the two women.

Jean got out first, leaving her sister alone in the cab with her new companion. The cab dropped them off around one, just yards away from Helen's home. But in the Puttock household, there was no sign of her arrival. Helen's husband George started to worry but was sure his wife would return that night.

Whenever she went out, she was always sure to return by the time her boys woke up in the morning. George stayed up worrying about his wife's failure to return home late into the evening but eventually fell asleep around two or three, figuring she must've stopped at Jean's house on her way.

A few hours later, a neighbor in Earls Street found Helen's body while walking his dog.

She was lying in the backcourt of the building, clothed, and seemingly strangled with a pair of tights. There was evidence of a struggle, Helen had some marks around her face and body, but not much more about the incident could be found from the scene.

When he awoke, George walked into the front room of his apartment and immediately saw a police van just up the road. He walked up to the van and asked the policeman if he could tell him what was going on—his wife had gone out last night and not returned home. The policeman immediately asked him what his wife had been wearing, when George described the clothes that had been found on the body, he was taken into the van and told that his wife had been murdered.

Helen Puttock hadn't been the first woman to die recently in Glasgow, but it was only after the discovery of her body that a pattern began to emerge. Twenty months earlier, on February 23, 1968, 25-year-old nurse Patricia Docker had gone dancing at the Barrowland and had also failed to return home. Her body was found the following morning. At the time, police suspected that it was just a typical murder case. They had no cause to suspect what was to come just over a year later.

The second victim of Bible John was found on August 16, 1968. Her name was Jemima McDonald. Her body was found by her sister and tenant just yards away from her home. Police found that plenty of people had seen McDonald at the Barrowland ballroom in the company of a male who was smartly dressed, aged somewhere between 25-35, with short blonde hair.

Witnesses gave such a good description of the man seen with McDonald that police were able to put together a composite sketch of the man they believed may have been the last to see her alive. Like Docker, she had been strangled. Ten weeks later, after Helen Puttock's body was found, these similarities became massively important.

Finding the man who had been in the taxi with Puttock and her sister became Glasgow police's top priority. After the case began to lose steam, George Puttock himself met with the taxi driver who had driven his wife to her death that fateful evening. The man had only been driving taxi's a couple of nights when he picked up Helen and Jean from the Barrowland, so he wasn't too familiar with the route to Puttock's house.

On his way there he had taken a wrong turn, making Helen irate. Instead of allowing the driver to fix his mistake, Helen insisted he stop the car where he was, saying she'd walk the rest of the way. The taxi driver then told George Puttock that the man accompanying Helen paid the fare and jumped out with her. He then grabbed Helen, who attempted to push the man off of him. The taxi driver, thinking he was witnessing nothing more than a lover's quarrel, drove off.

The details of Helen's murder brought a chilling echo of the deaths of the other two women. All three women had been dancing at the Barrowland and had been strangled by items of their own clothing near their homes the same night. The investigation into all three murders began with gusto because investigator's had a unique witness, Helen Puttock's sister Jean, who had spent time in the car with Helen and her murderer.

Investigators decided that Jean would be a good candidate to undergo hypnosis as a way of remembering details of that night. While under hypnosis, Jean was able to remember several details of the conversation the three dancers had had that night in the taxi. She knew the man's name was John, and that he extensively quoted from the Bible. She was also able to provide a detailed description of the man.

The police were so confident about Jean's detailed description that they commissioned the Glasgow School of Art to paint the portrait of the man they now called Bible John. The face would haunt Glasgow for years to come. When it was shown to Jean, she gave an involuntary gasp and stated that seeing the face again made her stomach turn. It seemed they had found their man.

Based on a statement of Jean's that Bible John had said he was in the military, the police began to interview soldiers who were home on leave at the time. Some thought he might have even been a police officer. Investigators interviewed thousands of men in several occupations all across the city but didn't seem to have any luck.

In what was one of the more unusual lines of inquiry, police officers were instructed to take to the dancefloor of the Barrowland to try and catch the killer stalking his next victim. While they were there, police also introduced themselves to as many women as possible, telling the women why they were there, and asking them to alert them if any strange man tried to take them home. Police also brought Jean with them to the Barrowland on several occasions, thinking that she would be able to identify the man herself if he was there. Nothing came of these efforts.

The more time passed, the more police began to worry that they had been putting too much faith in Jean's witness statements. If she had been wrong, they would have been looking in all the wrong places this whole time. They had initially believed that Jean was their slam dunk witness, someone who would instantly lead them to the man they were looking for, but so far they had found nothing.

The man in charge of the hunt for Bible John was a legendary Glaswegian investigator named Joe Beattie, but the case quickly became a challenge, even for him. Joe Beattie was a very dedicated officer who often worked long hours — at one point in the case, his coworkers described him as working almost 24-hours a day, seven days a week.

Beattie was so immersed in the case that he would tell his co-workers that if he came face to face with Bible John, he would be able to instantly recognize him from the many composite sketches and portraits that had been put together. He would rule out suspects on visual appearance alone.

Despite Beattie's hard work and great reputation, he never got the lucky break he needed to solve the case. Most of what Beattie had been investigating was based off of Jean's statements, which lost more credibility the longer the case went unsolved. Jean had been desperate to help find the man who killed her sister, but many began to suspect that in her desperate bid to help, Jean had tried to provide more information than she actually had.

But it wasn't only Jean who had gotten a good look at the man. The night he was with

Helen, Bible John had gotten the attention of several men working at the Barrowland by creating a fuss when Jean and Helen had trouble with a cigarette machine in the hall. The employees all agreed on their description of the man, but it countered the description given by Jean, further discrediting her original statements.

As the months and years passed, Glasgow police continued to hit dead end and dead end in their hunt for Bible John. At first, Glasgow seemed paralyzed by the idea that a serial killer was stalking their streets, but as time passed and no other victims were found, Bible John became a boogeyman figure for the city — someone used to scare children into having good behavior than a real figure to be feared.

In 1996, more than 30 years since Bible John's last victim was found, a new team of investigators took a second crack at the notorious cold case. New technology gave the team new hope for the first time in years. Among the evidence collected during the original investigation was a semen stain found on the clothes of one of the victims.

In the 60's, this was relatively useless to police, but in the late 90's it could be tested for DNA. In a decision that shocked many in Glasgow, the new team of investigators decided to exhume the body of John McInnes, a prime suspect in the case, who had committed suicide in 1980. The exhumation of McInnes's body is often seen as one of the grimmest moments in the search for Bible John. It recalled the days of horror during Scotland's body snatching years to many, and was seen as almost barbaric to most.

The exhumation was carried out early one cold morning in front of a barrage of journalists and onlookers fascinated with the macabre scene. The ground and tombstones of the graveyard were all covered in a heavy frost as the ground was broken on McInnes's grave. The coffin was dug out and moved to the city morgue in Glasgow.

Unfortunately, the DNA from the stain on the victim's clothing was so degraded by the time it was tested that DNA scientists could not determine one way or the other if the sample from the clothing and the sample from the exhumed body matched. Several years later after the further development of DNA technology, the samples were determined beyond a doubt to not match.

Faced with growing opposition towards the way they handled the case, the original team of investigators maintained that when the killer of Helen Puttock, Jemima McDonald, or Patricia Docker was found, he would be guilty of all three murders. More recently, investigators have concluded that it is likely that the crimes were committed by two or three separate individuals, all of whom may have been protected by the created personality of Bible John.

Despite modern investigators claiming that the notorious Bible John murders were most likely committed by separate individuals,

many people believe they were committed
by another one of Scotland's infamous serial
killers — Peter Tobin.

Peter Tobin - The Real Bible John?

Peter Tobin, born August 27, 1946 is a Scottish convicted serial killer and sex offender who is currently serving three life sentences in an Edinburgh prison as of 2016. Tobin has been convicted for the murders of three women between 1991 and 2006. Because of his criminal track record, many people, especially those who connect him with the Bible John murders, believe his total victim count is much higher than three.

Tobin was born and raised in Johnstone, a mid-sized town just West of Glasgow. From an early age, Tobin was aggressive and often got into trouble for causing fights amongst his seven brothers and sisters. When he was seven years old, Tobin's parents decided they could no longer handle his behaviors at home, so they sent him to an approved school.

Approved schools in Scotland were similar to borstals, but less strictly regulated. They were considered to be a preventative measure of reform as opposed to punishment for a crime. At his approved school, Tobin would have experienced a life not much different than any other child in a simple boarding school. At his young age he had yet to commit any offences, he was just too much of a handful for his overwhelmed parents. Tobin would spend time in young offender institutions later though, and by the time he was 24, Tobin was imprisoned in England for forgery and burglary.

Tobin spent most of his young adult life living in England. During this time, he acquired three ex-wives, three children, and a fourteen year prison sentence for the rape and attempted murder of two fourteen-year-old girls. On August 4, 1993, the girls had come the building Tobin lived in to visit his neighbor, but had arrived before their friend had returned home. They then made the mistake that almost caused them their life, they rang Tobin's apartment instead and asked if they could wait inside with him for their friend to return.

Once the girls entered his apartment, Tobin locked the doors and told the girls they wouldn't be leaving. He used a large kitchen knife to scare the young women into drinking large amounts of cider and vodka until they were clearly intoxicated. In this state, it was much easier for Tobin to control the girl's movements. He then raped the girls and stabbed them multiple times.

Tobin then left the apartment with his youngest son, who had shockingly been present for the attacks, expecting the girls to be dead when he returned. When he did return several hours later after returning his son to his mother, Tobin was surprised to see both of the girls had survived and managed to escape. Tobin hit the road, and evaded capture for seven months before he was eventually arrested in Brighton.

When Tobin was released from prison in September 2006 he was sixty years old, but he was not done with his life of crime just yet. He decided to move back to his hometown in Scotland and quickly found a job working as a handyman at the St. Patrick's Roman Catholic Church just outside of Glasgow.

Although he had been registered on the Violent and Sex Offender Register, which was accessible across the UK, Tobin had taken on an alias to avoid detection. His alias, Pat McLaughlin, also helped him avoid being arrested for an outstanding warrant he had for moving out of England without notifying the police.

On September 24, 2006, police were called to the St. Patrick's Roman Catholic Church where Tobin worked to investigate the disappearance of a young girl who had been living and working at the church over the summer. At the time, no one would have been able to guess where she would eventually turn up.

For many, church is a place of peace and tranquility. It certainly was for Angelika Kluk. The young Polish student was living and working at St. Patrick's over her summer break from University. No doubt in such surroundings she felt safe, no one could harm her inside the church, no one with any conscious at least.

But Tobin was different, and his depravity shocked even the toughest investigators. All of the lead detectives on the case would later describe the murder as the coldest; most brutal they had ever seen. One they would always remember.

Before he murdered Kluk, Tobin was well-trusted by the church's staff and regular attendees. He began helping out around the church before he worked there by assisting a local charity who used the church to feed the homeless population of Glasgow. Tobin would help the charity set up tables and even handed out meals.

He seemed like an upstanding citizen, often described as quiet, but very helpful. After being hired full-time as the church's only handyman, Tobin took on a greater role within the church. He became responsible for almost everything that happened in the church, and spent most of his days there.

When Kluk began working alongside him, she tragically caught his eye.

Kluk and Tobin worked alongside each other for months without a problem. The two got along well, and Kluk, a devoutly religious individual, appreciated all the hard work Tobin did to make sure the religious center ran smoothly and was kept well-maintenance. The pair was often seen chatting on the site, laughing. Kluk had fallen for Tobin's charm.

Late on September 23, 2006 Tobin found the perfect opportunity to show Kluk who he really was. The pair was working alone late that evening when Tobin hit Kluk in the back of her head with a table leg, rendering the young girl unconscious. This blow caused

Kluk's body to collapse to the ground. Tobin immediately bound, gagged, raped, and stabbed her.

After he had finished with Kluk, he wrapped her body in plastic bags, took her from the murder scene in the garage, and slid her to a small hole under the church's floor. He then went back to his business preparing the Sunday supper for the charity that earned him his job with the church in the first place. When the church filled up the next day, no one had any idea that Kluk's lifeless body lay just beneath their feet, or that her killer was sitting calmly amongst them.

The next day, with no trace of Kluk in sight, church staff reported her as missing to the police. When police arrived they interviewed all the church's staff, including calm and composed Tobin, who continued to use his alias Pat McLaughlin. Tobin had been busy that day erecting a shed on the church's grounds and was not thought to be a suspect after he was interviewed. What police failed to see when they were speaking to Tobin was that Kluk's blood was splattered on the wood boards Tobin was using as materials for the shed he was erecting.

Three days after Kluk was reported missing, she still hadn't been found, and Tobin stopped showing up for work at the church. Police launched a nationwide media appeal which named Pat McLaughlin as the last person to see her alive, alongside a recent picture of Peter Tobin. Luckily for police, an ex-neighbor of Tobin was watching the program and she recognized the face in the picture, but not the name. She immediately called police and told them that they were probably looking for the right man, but they had the wrong name. Pat McLaughlin was Peter Tobin.

After Tobin stopped showing up for work, police became suspicious. When they further learned that he had been using an alias since he moved back to Edinburgh, they immediately knew he must've been responsible for Kluk's disappearance.

Now all they needed to do was find him. He had completely abandoned his residence in Glasgow, and police feared he may have fled the country altogether. In reality, Tobin had left Glasgow for Edinburgh, and after spending the night there he moved further South to London, where he checked into a hospital using a fake name with a fake illness.

He had signed himself in as James Kelly, but luckily a staff member at the hospital recognized him as the man whose face was now being plastered on the news across the entire UK. The hospital worker immediately called the police.

On the same day that Tobin was discovered to be hiding in London, Kluk's body was discovered in the small hole beneath the church's floorboards. The investigators noted several facts about the body right away—her hands were severely blood-stained and her pants were undone. It was apparent from the second police laid eyes on her that Kluk had been the victim of a brutal assault.

It took less than a week for criminologists to isolate a DNA profile of the man they believed was Kluk's killer. Kluk had clearly been raped, and they were able to collect semen from both Kluk's body and clothing. When the profile was compared to profiles kept in a UK crime database, they matched with Tobin, whose DNA was on file from the rape and attempted murders he had committed back in 1993. Tobin was brought back to Glasgow for questioning, but denied any involvement. It was up to police to prove beyond a reasonable doubt that Tobin had committed the heinous crime.

Angelika Kluk's murder was so callous and so brutal it shocked the country. It was clear from the beginning that there was no way it could have been committed by a first time murderer. The cool, calculated way that he remained there and covered up his tracks indicated to investigators that he had committed a similar crime in the past. The police knew that if they were going to uncover how many other crimes Tobin had already committed, they were going to have to analyze every aspect of his mysterious past. They set up a unique, secret investigation team called Operation Anagram.

The team assigned to Operation Anagram took all the information they had about Tobin's past and broke it down by laying out where he had been when, and then looking at missing persons cases that came up in nearby areas. Tobin's entire life story could be found within the Operation Anagram's office walls.

Operation Anagram utilized information from every police force within the UK as Tobin moved between England and Scotland frequently throughout his life. His frequent travelling had made it difficult for police to keep track of his crimes and movements before, as each time he moved he crossed into another police unit's jurisdiction. Over his lifetime, Tobin also used over 40 aliases — a new one each time he moved. He was an individual who spent his entire free life acting like he had something to hide.

Operation Anagram built a criminal profile for Tobin based off of the information they were able to gather about his childhood and his behaviors as he developed into an antisocial, independent adult. They labelled him as a loner who could turn on an irresistible charm when needed, especially with vulnerable young women. What Anagram needed to do was figure out when he began to use his charm to lure victims into his deadly trap.

The Anagram detectives found that Tobin's first victims were his ex-wives. All three of Tobin's exes told police shocking stories of how he isolated them from their families and forced them to conform to his desires. His first wife spoke of how Tobin didn't allow her to leave his home for over a year, and each time he left he would lock her in a room.

One night when she didn't want to have sex, Tobin raped her and then sexually assaulted her wife a knife. He then left the woman for dead. When a neighbor discovered the woman after hearing her screams, an ambulance was called, and she survived the attack. She was then released back into Tobin's care and was forced to marry the man who had almost killed her just months later.

She only got away from Tobin after being jailed with him for being a potential accomplice in one of Tobin's many early cases for theft. When her mom arrived at the jail to bail her out, she explained to her what was happening. It was the first time she had seen her mother in over a year, and she used the opportunity to finally escape Tobin's possession.

This pattern of abuse continued throughout all three of Tobin's marriages. He physically and mentally abused his wives, but loved the children his second and third wife gave him. Despite enduring an unspeakable amount of abuse from Tobin, his second wife allowed him to visit with their son after she left him. She had been raised by her grandparents and had never known her own parents. She didn't want the same for her son.

To be closer to his boy, Tobin moved into a small house in Margate, and later an apartment in Havant, where he had raped and attempted to murder the two fourteen-year-old girls that won him his first long-term prison sentence. Tobin doted on his son and had never so much as spanked the young boy, so Tobin was allowed to have the boy over to stay overnight and on weekends in both his Margate house and Havant apartment. For Tobin, these visits with his son were the perfect excuse to have young women working as babysitters around.

The two residences in Margate and Havant became significant for investigators looking at Tobin's background. While he had already been charged for crimes he committed in his Havant apartment, they had yet to find any record of criminal activity committed while he lived in Margate. This made investigator's suspicious, so they decided to visit the property and complete a thorough search of the building and grounds. Investigators were not shocked, but dismayed, at what they found.

The skeletal remains of Vicky Hamilton, a young girl who was only fifteen years old when she went missing, were found buried in the property's back garden. Although Tobin denied killing the girl, investigators were able to confirm that Tobin had been the only one living in the property at the time of the girl's disappearance. Further, they were able to find evidence that countered his alibi, as well as DNA evidence and fingerprints that matched his own on Hamilton's personal belongings and the sheeting her body was wrapped in.

Operation Anagram would soon return to the Magrate house after they were given new leads surrounding the unsolved murder of Dinah McNicol. McNichol had gone missing from the area in 1991 after hitchhiking home from a music festival. She was last seen alive by her travelling companion who rode in the car with her for several miles before getting out.

After she disappeared, regular withdrawals were made from her bank account until it was completely drained. Because of this activity, police were unable to say for certain whether she was missing or if she had simply run off, although McNichol's family and friends adamantly protested that running away was not in McNichol's character. McNichol's disappearance wouldn't be solved until 2007, when Anagram detectives identified a second set of skeletal remains found on Tobin's old property as being McNichol herself.

With two previously unsolved murders under their belt, Operation Anagram continued digging into Peter Tobin's past to identify as many of his potential victims as possible. Fueled by a claim from Tobin's cellmate that he bragged about killing 48 women, the Operation's detectives worked relentlessly. Around 2009, detectives working under Anagram began to make a startling connection between Tobin and a series of earlier crimes that had been committed in Glasgow in 1968 and 1969 — the Bible John murders.

Peter Tobin had lived in Glasgow during the time of the Bible John murders, and had left suddenly in 1969, the same year the killings officially ended. This was consistent with the way Tobin had moved around the UK — he would find a new home generally within a month of each of his murders.

As well, many people have been able to see distinct similarities between Tobin's physical appearance of the time and many of the composite sketches the police had of the man they believed to be Bible John. When the Bible John investigation began to rely too heavily on the now thought to be incorrect artist's interpretation of the man, Tobin may have eluded capture as he lacked some key characteristics.

One undoubted characteristic that Tobin shares with the description of Bible John is the absence of a tooth in the upper-right corner of his mouth. This detail came up in several eye witness statements, and Anagram investigators were able to discover that Tobin had had a tooth removed on the upper-right side of his mouth in the late 1960's. He also had had a religious upbringing and frequently used aliases while committing crimes.

Although many people still desperate for a conclusion to the chilling case firmly believe that Peter Tobin is Bible John, Anagram investigators have never released an official statement either condemning the man as Bible John or clearing his name from the list of suspects.

Unfortunately, a semen stain that was recovered from the clothing of one of Bible John's victims is no longer able to be tested against new matches. The sample has severely deteriorated due to poor storage in the earlier portion of the Bible John investigation. This DNA was the same evidence used to clear John McInnes, the only other prime suspect in the case, of any wrongdoing.

Close

The small country of Scotland is world-renowned for its beautiful cities and stunning rural landscapes. It's hard to believe that this scenic and historical country could be the home of any wrongdoings. In 2015 however, the United Nations named Scotland as being one of the most dangerous countries globally, bringing new attention to Scotland's horrifying criminal past.

Scotland's modern history has been plagued with some of the most heinous crimes the world has ever seen. From the country's long history of body snatching, to the murder and sexual assault of children, and the unsolved serial killings that still haunt Glasgow today, Scotland's criminal history proves that even the most beautiful exterior cannot protect from the dark potential which plagues its inhabitants.